EAT LIKE A LOCAL- CLEVELAND

Cleveland Ohio Food Guide

Shannon Brennan

Eat Like a Local-Cleveland Copyright © 2021 by CZYK Publishing LLC. All Rights Reserved.

All rights reserved. No part of this book may be reproduced in any form or by any electronic or mechanical means including information storage and retrieval systems, without permission in writing from the author. The only exception is by a reviewer, who may quote short excerpts in a review.

The statements in this book are of the authors and may not be the views of CZYK Publishing.

Cover designed by: Lisa Rusczyk Ed. D.

CZYK Publishing Since 2011.

Eat Like a Local

Lock Haven, PA
All rights reserved.
ISBN: 9798597842066

BOOK DESCRIPTION

Are you excited about planning your next trip? Do you want an edible experience? Would you like some culinary guidance from a local? If you answered yes to any of these questions, then this Eat Like a Local book is for you. Culinary tourism is an important aspect of any travel experience. Food has the ability to tell you a story of a destination, its landscapes, and culture on a single plate. Most food guides tell you how to eat like a tourist. Although there is nothing wrong with that, as part of the Eat Like a Local series, this book will give you a food guide from someone who has lived at your next culinary destination.

In these pages, you will discover advice on having a unique edible experience. This book will not tell you exact addresses or hours but instead will give you excitement and knowledge of food and drinks from a local that you may not find in other travel food guides.

Eat like a local. Slow down, stay in one place, and get to know the food, people, and culture. By the time you finish this book, you will be eager and prepared to travel to your next culinary destination.

OUR STORY

Traveling has always been a passion of the creator of the Eat Like a Local book series. During Lisa's travels in Malta, instead of tasting what the city offered, she ate at a large fast-food chain. However, she realized that her traveling experience would have been more fulfilling if she had experienced the best of local cuisines. Most would agree that food is one of the most important aspects of a culture. Through her travels, Lisa learned how much locals had to share with tourists, especially about food. Lisa created the Eat Like a Local book series to help connect people with locals which she discovered is a topic that locals are very passionate about sharing. So please join me and: Eat, drink, and explore like a local.

Eat Like a Local

TABLE OF CONTENTS

BOOK DESCRIPTION
OUR STORY
TABLE OF CONTENTS
ABOUT THE AUTHOR
HOW TO USE THIS BOOK
FROM THE PUBLISHER
1. The Great Divide
2. Where to Stay
3. Gettin' Around
4. When to Visit
5. Photo Op
6. Coffee Shops
7. Start Your Day the Right Way
8. A Venue with a View
9. Super Little Soup Shop
10. Family Owned Falafel
11. Hold the Meat!
12. Big Appetites Only
13. Wingin' It!
14. Succulent Sushi
15. Dinner and a Drink
16. Smoky Flavors and Sticky Fingers
17. Drive In to the Blast from the Past
18. Hot Diggity Dog!

19. Breweries and Wine Bars
20. See you Lager!
21. All Roads Lead to BEER!
22. Relax with the Perfect Glass
23. Pockets of Night Life
24. The Flats
25. West 6th Downtown
26. West End Lakewood
27. A City Of Immigrants
28. Italia Autentica
29. When Irish Eyes are Smiling
30. Savory Spices
31. Tacos For Days
32. All Around Asia
33. Best Burgers
34. Battle Royale
35. Treats and Trains
36. Lake Erie is Great
37. Less Beach, More Lake
38. Hikin' and Bikin'
39. A Park for Picasso's
40. Fall in Love with the Falls
41. Food Trucks
42. Explore the Shopping Scene
43. Feeding the Body and the Soul
44. Plates and Punch Lines

45. End the Day on Broadway
46. Freeze Baby
47. Donut Forget the Donuts!
48. Cute Lil' (or Big) Cupcakes
49. To All the Chocoholics
50. A Town Willy Wonka Would Be Proud Of

READ OTHER BOOKS BY
CZYK PUBLISHING

ABOUT THE AUTHOR

You won't find a truer Clevelander than Shannon, the author of this guide. Born and raised in the CLE, Shannon has lived in 8 of the different neighborhoods and suburbs of Cleveland in the course of the last ten years. Calling so many areas "home" has made her an expert on all things food and entertainment in the city of Cleveland. She also married a local Clevelander, whose expertise has played a huge role in the creation of this guide.

A graduate of Cleveland State University, Shannon is currently an English teacher at a local high school in the area, She is the oldest of 8 siblings, who all live within 15 minutes of each other. Outside of investigating the hidden secrets of Cleveland, Shannon enjoys reading, running and listening to podcasts while taking long walks along Lake Erie.

Shannon also has experience as a traveller in many places throughout the United States and abroad. She hopes that this book will help travellers have an experience that leaves them inspired and that it showcases the strengths of her often overlooked but beautiful home.

HOW TO USE THIS BOOK

The goal of this book is to help culinary travelers either dream or experience different edible experiences by providing opinions from a local. The author has made suggestions based on their own knowledge. Please do your own research before traveling to the area in case the suggested locations are unavailable.

Travel Advisories: As a first step in planning any trip abroad, check the Travel Advisories for your intended destination.
https://travel.state.gov/content/travel/en/traveladvisories/traveladvisories.html

Eat Like a Local

FROM THE PUBLISHER

Traveling can be one of the most important parts of a person's life. The anticipation and memories that you have are some of the best. As a publisher of the *Eat Like a Local*, Greater Than a Tourist, as well as the popular *50 Things to Know* book series, we strive to help you learn about new places, spark your imagination, and inspire you. Wherever you are and whatever you do I wish you safe, fun, and inspiring travel.

Lisa Rusczyk Ed. D.
CZYK Publishing

Eat Like a Local

"There comes a time in every rightly constructed boy's life when he has a raging desire to go somewhere and dig for hidden treasure."

Mark Twain

Cleveland, Ohio is not always the up and coming destination that tops most travellers lists. Many might think that there is little to do and see here, but I hope to change their minds by the end of this guide. This historical port town that borders the Great Lake Erie is one of those "hidden treasures" Mark Twain refers to. Over the last few decades, Clevelanders have put their hearts and souls into revitalizing this city, and today's out of town guests will definitely notice the fruits of the local's labors.

Dining is a highlight, and sometimes even the main attraction, of any worthwhile trip. The cuisine of a city not only fuels its people, but its culture as well. People share their stories through food. Whether that be the story of their heritage, the story of their family or the story of their dreams, people often express themselves by sharing food with others. The eclectic combination of unique food options here in Cleveland tells you just how diverse and thriving this city really is. If you're lucky, by the time you leave, you will get to hear someone's story firsthand.

This book is a collection of my best recommendations and those of all the proud, local friends and family who I surveyed for this project. I hope you will find these tips helpful, and that you decide to pay this passionate and energizing city a visit!

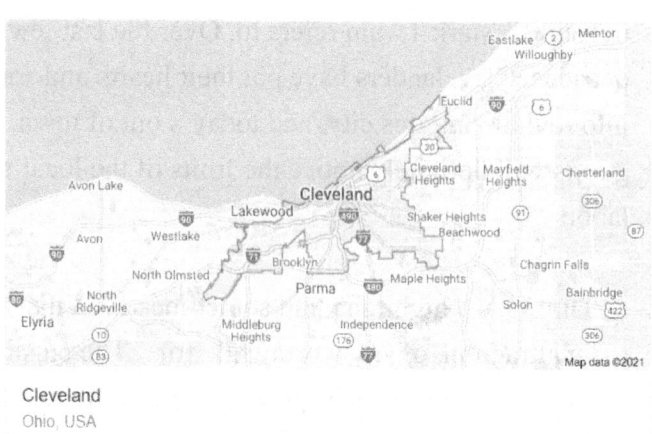

Cleveland
Ohio, USA

Eat Like a Local

Cleveland Ohio Climate

	High	Low
January	34	23
February	37	24
March	45	31
April	57	42
May	68	53
June	77	63
July	81	68
August	80	67
September	74	61
October	63	50
November	52	39
December	40	29

GreaterThanaTourist.com

Temperatures are in Fahrenheit degrees.
Source: NOAA

1. THE GREAT DIVIDE

Before I start with my culinary clues, I think it's important to give you a little background on the geography of the Cleveland area. There is plenty to do in central Downtown to keep you busy, but venturing a little outside central Cleveland is also worth your while. There are many neighborhoods right outside of downtown that are still considered within the Cleveland city limits, and then there are suburbs that are considered their own entity. These neighborhoods/suburbs are not far; everything that I put in this book can be reached within half an hour of leaving central downtown. However, to keep it clear, Clevelanders think of themselves as separated into two main groups: East Siders (those who live East of Downtown) and West Siders (those who live West of Downtown). As I go through the rest of this book, if you see a mention to the East or West Side, that is what I mean. I have attached a little guide below of places I mention in this book and what side of the city they are on.

- Cleveland Neighborhoods (within city limits of Cleveland)
- Central Downtown & the Flats
- Ohio City (A little west)
- Tremont (A little west)
- Kamm's Corner (A little west)
- Gordon Square (A little west)
- University Circle (A little east)
- West Side Suburbs
- Lakewood
- Fairiview
- Westlake
- Rocky River
- Bay Village
- Avon
- East Side Suburbs
- Cleveland Heights/University Heights
- Chagrin Falls
- Euclid

2. WHERE TO STAY

Both the East and West Sides of Cleveland have plenty to offer in terms of food and excursions, so in terms of places to set up home base, I would suggest something central. If you're looking for something higher end, a downtown hotel, such as the 9 or the Wyndham, will offer you the luxury city experience you are looking for. If you're on a tight budget, or would just rather stay a little outside the city, I would recommend looking at AirBnb. For the best combination of safe, high quality, and convenient, I would suggest looking at AirBnb's in either Tremont, Ohio City or Lakewood. These Cleveland neighborhoods still have that urban feel but offer a little distance from the city. They also give you a better image of the culture of the Cleveland area, with the added perk of much more convenient parking.

3. GETTIN' AROUND

If you are planning a trip to Cleveland and hoping to get a true "taste" of the area (both literally and figuratively), I would suggest having access to a car, either by driving your own for your trip, or renting a car once you arrive. Most everywhere has access to parking, either metered or in parking garages. Honestly, in many of the surrounding neighborhoods downtown, parking is free on side streets. Additionally, the traffic is very manageable for the most part. If having a car is not an option for you, the RTA bus system is available; however, to really make the most of your time, having a car is your best bet.

4. WHEN TO VISIT

While the Cleveland winters are somewhat of a legend, to truly get a taste of everything Cleveland has to offer, the best time to visit is between May and October. You're almost guaranteed the weather for outdoor experiences, and are able to take advantage of the lake, which is much too cold for activities in the winter. In addition to the lake experience, many parks and restaurants (Lakewood Park, Edgewater Park, Cain Park and the Westlake Rec Center) have free concerts that run in the summer which can be a no cost way to spend an evening. If you're planning a trip to Cleveland, summer days are the way!

***Bonus Note: I should mention that if you love Irish culture or are looking for a bustling and action packed trip, St. Patricks Day is always a party here in Cleveland. It's still pretty cold here in March, but Clevelanders find a way to make it work!

5. PHOTO OP

If you love a good instagram shot and want to have yourself a free scavenger hunt during your visit, Cleveland has its own little adventure built in for you with the recently installed Cleveland script signs. The locals love to stop at these picture perfect hidden gems and grab a solo shot or a nice group picture. Strategically placed in areas that highlight some of Cleveland's most scenic backdrops, making a stop at all, or even just one, of these cute, stand out structures will give you a picture to show your friends when you return back home. The locations of the five Cleveland script signs are listed below:

- North Coast Harbor, 9th Street Pier (Downtown)
- Edgewater Park (Lakewood)

- The Flats (Downtown)
- Abbey Avenue (Right Outside Downtown)
- Euclid Beach Park (Euclid)

Now that you know a little bit about the city in general, onto the food!

6. COFFEE SHOPS

Coffee shops are the hidden gems of every city. Nothing hits the spot quite like a quality cup of the good stuff, on a warm summer's day or in the middle of one of our chilly winters. The best place to stop here in Cleveland for your caffeine fix would be one of the branches of Phoenix Coffee Co. Phoenix branches are located in the downtown area and the east side and they provide quaint seating and high quality, locally roasted coffee, Phoenix Coffee Co is my favorite place to grab a quick drink or to catch up on some work.

If you are gravitating more towards the West Side, I would recommend giving Root Cafe a shot. This community hotspot is known for its passion for organic, vegetarian ingredients and the staff is always friendly and welcoming. This coffee shop also is not only a place for warm and cold brews, it also showcases and sells projects from local artists around the Cleveland area. This is a great place for a laid back date or a meeting with a friend.

Energize your travels with a cup of joe from one of these quaint cafes!

7. START YOUR DAY THE RIGHT WAY

They say breakfast is the most important meal of the day, and there's no reason to ignore that little token of wisdom just because you are out of town. There's no better spot for breakfast than in the earthy neighborhood of Tremont, located right outside of Downtown. This neighborhood is an eclectic mix of old, historical homes and chic new apartment buildings, which brings a healthy mix of people to the area. It is also home to many quaint restaurants and bars that lie on its academically themed streets like Professor Drive and Literary Road. But in my opinion, the best time of the day to hit Tremont is for breakfast. However, you will be forced to make the tough choice between the two most delicious breakfast hotpots: Luckys Cafe and Grumpys Cafe.

Luckys Cafe, located on Starkweather Avenue, is a small brick establishment that prides itself on being a local business that sources its ingredients from other local farms and businesses in the Greater Cleveland Area. WIth its small but specialized menu, Luckys offers their take on breakfast and lunch classics, and they won't overwhelm you with a 5 page menu. If you want an insider's tip on what to order, give the Waffles or the Curried Chicken Salad Sandwich a shot.

Grumpys Cafe is located just a few blocks over on West 14th Street. This cozy, family friendly cafe offers both breakfast and lunch comfort food, which they love to say, "will never leave you grumpy" (how punny of them). The restaurant offers both indoor and outdoor seating year round and prides themselves on their quick, yet welcoming service. A little different than Luckys, Grumpys has an all encompassing menu, including eggs, omelettes, pancakes, waffles, sandwiches, salads, and much

Eat Like a Local

more. My Grumpys favorites would have to be their killer omelettes.

Whichever you choose, Tremont is sure to satisfy your breakfast needs!

8. A VENUE WITH A VIEW

Cliff diving? How about cliff dining! Pier W is a high end restaurant in Lakewood that is actually built into the side of a cliff! I surveyed many friends while writing this book, and 90% of them agreed: a food guide on Cleveland would not be complete without an entry on Pier W. From the moment you approach Pier W, the secret looking entrance to the restaurant will really make you feel like you've found a local hidden gem. This establishment's specialty is seafood and is ideal for a special celebration dinner, but if you are really looking for their A game, the brunch is an absolute must. Not only is food incredible, this view of the lake in the morning will take your breath away.

9. SUPER LITTLE SOUP SHOP

Soup lovers unite at my personal favorite little hole in the wall known as The Souper Market. Perfect for vegetarian, vegan, gluten free and endless other diets, this easy to miss little shop has something for everyone. The employees are always incredibly friendly and they always offer great variety. My personal favorite is the chicken paprikash soup, combined with the green apple salad. While I'd pay a million bucks for a meal like this one, it does make it taste even better that it's such a bargain as well. With locations in Lakewood, Ohio City and Kamms Corner, a pop into The Souper Market would be a great quick and easy lunch adventure!

10. FAMILY OWNED FALAFEL

Falafel and books. The perfect combo.

Okay, maybe that's not the first pairing that would come to your mind, but that is the dynamic duo that Tommy's Restaurant on Coventry in Cleveland Heights has to offer. Tommy's is family owned and you can feel that whenever you eat there...they truly make you feel like you belong, whether you stop everyday or its your first time. This restaurant , which is paired with a bookstore, has both meat and vegetarian options, but its specialty is hands down their falafel wraps. Unless we're counting desserts, in which case I'd have to change my mind and say their specialty is the milkshakes. I'm not one for ordering dessert with dinner, but I always find myself making an exception for a Tommy's milkshake. My favorite way to make a visit to Tommy's is to account for a little time to browse the conjoined Mac's Backs Bookstore before dinner....nothing like finding a good book before a good meal!

11. HOLD THE MEAT!

The family owned Cleveland Vegan, located in Lakewood, is an absolute staple for anyone on a vegan diet, or anyone who wants to experiment with something new. Owned by a well known local musician and his wife, the passion for vegan eating that this shop emanates is contagious. There is also no lack of creativity here; even though everything on the menu at this restaurant is vegan, their names may not seem like it. Menu items like gyros, "chicken" sandwiches, reubens, milkshakes and much more, all free of any animal products, have sparked my curiosity many a time and brought me into the Cleveland Vegan, never to be disappointed. I would especially recommend taking a sweet, sweet treat with you on your way out; their bakery is exquisite!

12. BIG APPETITES ONLY

After a big day of seeing the sights, you might find yourself ready to eat a horse. If you're looking for both quality and quantity, then add Melt Bar and Grilled to your itinerary. Melt Bar and Grill features experimental gourmet grilled cheese sandwiches of every shape but just one size: massive. These specialty sandwiches are big enough to satisfy the hungriest and the restaurant was even featured on an episode of Man vs. Food. Its TV debut was not the restaurant's only claim to fame; this Cleveland grown business was also featured in USA Today and Esquire as serving some of the best sandwiches in America! A must try for every hungry sandwich slugger!

13. WINGIN' IT!

My husband says the same thing every night in response to our dinner plans: wings! After trying Dina's Pizza & Pub, I think you all will agree with him after downing a delicious dozen at this Cleveland restaurant. Operating out of Old Brooklyn, Dina's has been the talk of the town with their award winning sauces and wings. But that's not all! If you are not in the wing mood, they have burgers, pizza, pasta, and other tasty options. One could say Dina's is a one stop shop for any type of heavenly fried gold! If you do go though, make sure to buy House Mild Wings with a side of zucchini fries and ranch. The way I see it, from a nutrition standpoint they "cancel" each other out!

14. SUCCULENT SUSHI

Cleveland, the sushi capital of the world?! That's sure how it feels after indulging in an all you can eat sushi buffet at Kintaro Hot Pot and Sushi. At a can't beat price you and your fellow vagabonds can share your hopes and dreams over quality sashimi and specialty rolls. Visiting with people who prefer their food to be cooked opposed to raw and rolled? First, be sure to shame those uncultured swine! Then assure them they will find plenty of menu items to enjoy, including all you can eat hibachi and hot pot options! With a few locations around the area, this must stop spot is easy to work into your Cleveland itinerary.

15. DINNER AND A DRINK

I could talk for days about the ambiance, the beverage selection and the prime location of McNulty's Bier Markt and Bar Cento. But I value your time and know you're someone who wants to get right to the point. WHEN YOU COME TO CLEVELAND YOU MUST ORDER THE POMMES FRITES AT BAR CENTO AND SHARE THE DELICACY WITH SOMEONE YOU LOVE! Garnished with whole garlic cloves and paired with three speciality dips, this dish will have you wondering what you did to deserve such a delicious meal. If I haven't sold you yet, (tough crowd), the ambiance of a chic pub, lengthy beer and cocktail list and location directly across from a famous Cleveland landmark, The West Side Market, should drive the point home. Let me just finish by saying, if Guy Fieri was coming to Cleveland I wouldn't let his frosted tips anywhere near this gem, I'm saving it just for you!

16. SMOKY FLAVORS AND STICKY FINGERS

Picture a Sunday afternoon in July. You just spent the day at Edgewater Beach and you've worked up quite an appetite. A day like this sounds like one that must end with a classic barbecue. If you're not looking to head out to the grill on your vacation, Landmark Smokehouse and Bar can do the dirty work for you. Located on Clifton Boulevard, right on the cusp of where Lakewood meets Cleveland, this relaxed barbecue joint is the perfect way to get a taste of that summertime feel in any season. Not to mention that is only a stone's throw from Edgewater Park, making it a great way to pair up your experiences. I personally prefer to hit Landmark for their brunch with a smokehouse twist!

17. DRIVE IN TO THE BLAST FROM THE PAST

When King James had once roamed these borders, he liked to stop at his Akron favorite: Swenson's Drive-In. The restaurant is not only located in Akron; Swenson's has multiple locations throughout Northeast Ohio. Bringing back the flavor of 1950's car dining, Swenson's has been around since the Great Depression (est. 1934)! That's a long time to be serving some of the best burgers, milkshakes, and specialty soft drinks around the area! As you arrive in the parking lot, it will seem as though a cross country meet is happening. No worries! Curbside waiters dash out to the customers car in order to greet, take the order, and serve them their food! When you find a parking spot, sit back and grab a menu from a waiter. The perfect combination to order: The Galley Boy, Potato Teezers (side of ranch always), and a small Ohio Specialty to drink. You are probably wondering what a specialty soft drink is, so here is

Eat Like a Local

my take. Swenson's has three: the Ohio, Florida, and California. They all correlate with fruits that are grown within those states. Ohio has cherries, Florida has oranges, and California has grapes. Essentially, it is a ginger ale with fruit flavor added in! Be sure to order any one and experience two states in one trip! Finally, as you are digging into this wonderful local treat, have some Fats Domino or Elvis Presley playing and you will truly embody the spirit of a youngster in the 1950's.

18. HOT DIGGITY DOG!

Ketchup, mustard, onions, sauerkraut, or relish. These are all toppings on one of America's favorite staples at a barbeque: the hot dog. However, have you ever wanted to explore what other options could be put on these treasures of the grill? Maybe peanut butter? Froot Loops? Well, at Happy Dog, one can start to conquer their wonder on what could go on a hot dog. If you find yourself in Gordon Square, follow the "mustard yellow" brick road to the restaurant to start your endeavor! Happy Dog has that feel of a neighborhood corner bar where you know everyone and it welcomes you with beer and food! Additionally, the bar has great live music. They showcase Cleveland's local music scene every weekend, so don't miss out on an opportunity to see a future inductee into the Rock and Roll Hall of Fame! Now, back to the dogs. With 4 different styles of hot dog and 50 toppings to choose from, you can get crazy with the toppings. Typical garnishes are on the menu, of course, but you are reading this for the outlandish ones! Besides the two mentioned, Happy Dog offers Cheetos, Spaghetti-O's, Everything Bagel Cream Cheese, and many others to allow you to feel like you are the Dr. Frankenstein of frankenfurters!

19. BREWERIES AND WINE BARS

A little known fact is the Cleveland area is teeming with breweries and wineries. Cleveland has over 40 total breweries who craft their beer in house. From porters, to hefeweizens, to sours and everything in between, Cleveland can satisfy even the most experienced beer connoisseur. Less prominent but no lower in quality, Cleveland is also home to many popular wineries. Both close to the city and a little farther out, Cleveland doesn't forget to satisfy all you wine lovers out there. With so many options to choose from, it may be overwhelming to choose a brewery or winery at random. The next few tips will highlight the best of the best.

20. SEE YOU LAGER!

The man. The myth. The legend.

Great Lakes Brewery is Cleveland's most popular brewery, and is an icon of the city as a whole. Buckle up for some more fun facts here! This brewery was the first brewpub in Ohio. Its owners took a risk and built it in the once struggling neighborhood of Ohio City. The brewery found great success, and this success inspired the revival of the whole neighborhood. Now, Ohio City is one of the most action packed and thriving neighborhoods of Cleveland.

Now that the history lesson is over, a little more on the Great Lakes experience. This combination of brewery and pub is the perfect place for a relaxed dinner or for just having a couple drinks. If you want to make an excursion out of it, the establishment offers tours of their brewery, that will give you an inside scoop on the brewing process and a little more info about the rich history of the organization and the neighborhood. Finally, I can't end this entry without throwing in a recommendation so here it is: If you are looking to try a Great Lakes classic, the Dortmunder Lager is their best seller, and a staple at any local Cleveland get together. However, if you are lucky enough to be at Great Lakes when they have Conway's Irish Ale on tap, I wait all year for this little treat, so take the opportunity to give it a shot!

21. ALL ROADS LEAD TO BEER!

Great Lakes Brewery set the bar high when they introduced their brews to the area of Cleveland. However, in 2011, Market Garden decided to add a little rivalry to see who has the best beer in town! If you have stuck around in Ohio City after your Great Lakes visit, then you are a stone's throw from the brewpub. Unlike Great Lakes' old school pub appeal,

Eat Like a Local

Market Garden brings a more modern, industrial feel to the people who enter the confines of the bar and restaurant. It is a perfect place to grab a bite to eat with a significant other! Also, if you are with a group of people, it will handle your needs. A friend of my husband had a small wedding dinner there that consisted of 13 people and the service was excellent! Similarly, it's not just the service that is excellent, it's the drinks! All beers on tap are made from their brewery, which is located right behind it. Just look for the enormous BEER! sign! Tours are available to the public, so give a quick call to see when you can schedule one.

My personal recommendation is their Prosperity Wheat (they offer IPA's, pilsners, etc. as well). This Bavarian-style Hefeweizen will tingle your taste buds! They sell six-packs of their beers on their website, so stock up while you are in town and don't pay shipping fees! If you do take a sixer of Prosperity home with you, then be sure to make a colaweizen. A mixture of cola and hefeweizen, the drink is oddly delicious and you can boast to your friends about what Cleveland has taught you!

22. RELAX WITH THE PERFECT GLASS

CLE Urban WInery is one of Cleveland's only wineries located within 20 minutes of downtown that actually crafts its wine in house. This relaxing yet energizing establishment capitalizes on its unique position as one of the few places that is actually creating wine in house at their urban location on Lee Road. To get the skinny on how they are pulling this off, take a tour of its facilities, or just schedule yourself a wine tasting and watch the action through their customer viewing window. I have found that CLE Urban Winery is a chic and soothing place to meet up and chat with a few friends. The seating is a combination of couches and regular tables, and the environment feels very laid back. An added bonus is you are permitted to bring outside food into the Winery, and the Cedar Lee Road area is swarming with great places for food, some of which are even willing to deliver the food to the winery for you. If you're looking for a way to unwind after a long day, venture over to CLE Urban Winery!

Eat Like a Local

23. POCKETS OF NIGHT LIFE

You may have come for the food, but you'll stay for the partayyy. If you're hoping to swig some libations after dinner, there are quite a few locations that will offer a pocket of the night life. Choose a location that's close enough to walk from where you're staying or call yourself an inexpensive Uber or a Lyft, but once you get to a spot, you'll be able to bar hop from any of these starting points.

24. THE FLATS

It was once called a Scooby Doo ghost town. Now, it is one of the prime spots to be for a great night and sights! Let's start off with your food options because that's the most important, right? Riddled with restaurants, like Beerhead, Dante's Inferno, or even Margaritaville, The Flats offers food that will leave you craving for more! Perfect! Dinner is settled now. Should we talk about some drinks? Head on over to Collision Bend Brewery or Landshark Rooftop Bar. Collision Bend crafts their own beers, so if you are a beer snob, you will fall in love. Both of these bars are great in the summer! With seating by the river and a gorgeous sunset, I think you should stay for at least one more drink. Finally, you have had enough of beer and food, so you want to have some fun. Check out the Big Bang Dueling Piano Bar or Punch Bowl Social. The Big Bang offers a fun, energetic atmosphere with piano players dueling out their takes on songs from all decades. Then again, maybe you are not in the mood for live music. Ah ha! Go to Punch Bowl Social instead! It holds a bowling alley, bar, and restaurant that will definitely serve as the perfect way to unwind after dinner.

25. WEST 6TH DOWNTOWN

So you have gone to the Flats, now what? Well, head east on to West 6th and find yourself entangled with the fantastic nightlife! The street comes alive deep into the night with the bass of music and flashes of light. West 6th employs a variety of clubs and restaurants that will have you poppin' bottles to the break of dawn! Check out local spots like Barley House, Dive Bar, The Velvet Dog, or Panini's. The

Velvet Dog is personally one of my recommendations, especially during the summer! With a rooftop bar and lots of space, it can cool off any one of those hot nights!

26. WEST END LAKEWOOD

If you want to get a taste of the night life, but are looking for an experience a little more low key than the lively Flats or Downtown Scene, take yourself down to the West End of Lakewood. This little collection of bars offers a vibrant taste of the nightlife, just on a much smaller scale with easier access to parking. Bar hop from the saloon style Around the Corner, over to the little hole in the wall Riverside, or maybe take a stop at the area's namesake West End Tavern...the options are endless and all within walking distance. All of these locations offer traditional bar grub and are very reasonably priced. However, I have to say, what draws me to West End, Lakewood for the night out is the dream of ending the party with a warm gooey cookie from Insomnia Cookies, which is open until the wee hours of the night for anyone with a midnight sweet tooth.

27. A CITY OF IMMIGRANTS

Cleveland is a melting pot of rich ethnic backgrounds. People are very proud of their culture's here, and one of the most prominent ways they show this is by sharing their food with the community. There are loads of authentic and unique restaurants from cultures around the world that are a must see of a trip to Cleveland. These restaurant's are scattered throughout the city, but in some cases, a bunch of them are condensed in a single area. Either choose a favorite or bounce around to a few but no matter what, Cleveland's ethnically diverse food options will not disappoint! Explore the next few tips for some recommendations of the highlights.

28. ITALIA AUTENTICA

If you are craving some authentic Italian classics, Cleveland's Little Italy is the best place to quench your cravings. Located on the East Side of Cleveland directly off of University Circle, this little collection of Italian restaurants is a favorite spot of many local Clevelanders. Whether you choose to treat yourself

Eat Like a Local

to some pasta at Trattoria, grab a quick slice of pizza at Mama Santa's or snag yourself a cannoli to-go at Presti's Bakery, a trip to Little Italy will satisfy all of your needs in its half mile stretch of quaint restaurants, bars and coffee shops. Also, if you are really looking to make an afternoon of it, make the walk up the steep hill on Mayfield and you will discover Cleveland's historical and scenic Lakeview Cemetery. The resting place of President James A. Garfield and an assortment of monuments, Lakeview Cemetery is a great place for a peaceful and educational stroll. A combination of these two Cleveland highlights is a worthwhile way to spend an afternoon or evening for all ages!

29. WHEN IRISH EYES ARE SMILING

Cleveland is known to be a hub for Irish immigrants, my grandmother being one of them, and they have made their presence known through their pubs and restaurants. Some of the most popular and entertaining of these pubs are the ones that host Cleveland's local Irish bands. These bands play many traditional Irish classics, and sometimes even music they have composed on their own. The groups Mary's Lane, New Barleycorn, and the Portersharks always put on a crowd pleasing show. If you're lucky, you might catch an Irish dancer or two performing, especially if you are visiting around St. Patrick's Day. As an Irish dancer myself, you may even catch me popping onto a stage for a little impromptu reel or jig session! There are so many options to choose from when it comes to restaurants that showcase Irish culture, that it's almost impossible for me to tailor them down, but if I have to I would suggest P.J. McCintyre's on Kamm's Corner (looks just like a pub in Ireland), Flannery's on 4th Street Downtown or Plank Tavern in Lakewood. A night at one of Cleveland's Irish pubs is one that will leave you smiling!

30. SAVORY SPICES

The colors. The textures. Most importantly the spices. Indian food is a unique combination of all three. Whether you're craving a Spicy Chicken Curry or are hoping for a classic Tikka Masala, you can find a mouthwatering execution of all of your favorite Indian dishes at Tandoul in the Tremont neighborhood of Cleveland. Tandoul offers a classy sit down dining experience, and can be a perfect place for a celebration dinner or date night. Furthermore, you can round it out taking a nice walk around Tremont, one of Cleveland's most up and coming areas. Taking a picture at the gazebo at the center of Lincoln Park, or stopping at one of the local bars can be a great follow up to your Indian cuisine experience. Try old favorites or try something new, but try it at Tandoul in Tremont!

31. TACOS FOR DAYS

If you are getting tired of the late night Taco Bell runs, then try these restaurants that will surely hit the (taco) spot! First, if you are looking for a dine in experience, you will have to try Barrio. The restaurant(s) are located in a few of Cleveland's surrounding neighborhoods: Lakewood, Tremont, Cleveland Heights, and even Downtown Cleveland. This restaurant has become somewhat of an icon here and will undoubtedly make you think twice about ordering that $1 bean burrito.

However, maybe you are in a rush and can't sit down? No worries. La Plaza Tacos can help you with your busy day. Situated on the border of Cleveland and Lakewood, La Plaza will give you authentic street tacos and a variety of other made to order items. Originally just a food stand within a grocery store, the news of their fabulous tacos have spread so much, they needed to expand. They are still located within the La Plaza Supermarket, but can be found in their own area which you will see right upon entering the supermarket. An added bonus is that you can also explore the Hispanic supermarket to look for other treats!

These two restaurants will give you something to "taco" bout when you return from your trip from Cleveland.

Eat Like a Local

32. ALL AROUND ASIA

Offering both traditional and non-traditional approaches, Cleveland has many restaurants that can provide an Asian inspired experience. For a traditional take on Thai cuisine, check out Brown Sugar Thai, with locations in both Rocky River and Lakewood. Brown Sugar Thai's mission is to bring a little bit of Thailand to Cleveland, and it does so with its authentic dishes and decor. Brown Sugar Thai is also a great option for all you health nuts out there (something I'm always on the lookout for), as its dishes include hearty vegetables and most of their meat items are not breaded or fried. Good for both dine in and takeout, Brown Sugar Thai is a flexible dinner option for your trip.

In contrast, Ninja City, located in Gordon Square, is a more eclectic take on some Asian inspired classics. They label themselves as Pan-Asian, so their dishes are inspired by foods from different countries all across Asia. Offering everything from curries, to Vietnamese Noodles to Korean Pork bowls, there's a little bit of everything here at Ninja City. With its hip, urban location in the Gordon Square District, Ninja

City not only offers satisfying food but also a satisfying environment.

Check out Cleveland's Asian inspired experience during your visit!

33. BEST BURGERS

Seeking a sizzling medium rare American classic? You know I'm talking about a good old fashioned burger, and you better believe you can find the best here. Almost every restaurant is going to offer their take but if you are looking for the true, award winning experts, visit either Hecks Cafe or Gunselmann's Tavern. Heck's Cafe has two locations, one in the urban Ohio City and the other in the more suburban surrounding suburb of Avon. The founding location in Ohio City is housed in a 120 year old brick townhouse, giving it an antique and historical ambiance. The Avon location is more modern, with a sleek warehouse vibe. Both locations offer indoor and outdoor seating, and a burger you will never forget. Just the other day, my husband and I ordered two of our personal favorites: the Au

Eat Like a Local

Cheval Burger (a classic fried egg burger) and the more experimental BrieBerry Burger (a bacon cheeseburger topped with a blueberry sauce).

A community favorite, Gunselmann's tavern is a burger joint located in Fairview, a West Side suburb of Cleveland. The building where the magic happens is a very unique looking seven sided brick building that is actually an old speakeasy, and you can just feel the rich history from the moment you walk into the place. Less experimental than Hecks but no lower in quality, Gunselmanns features classic burger combinations, with my personal favorite being the straight forward Gunny Barbeque Bacon. The restaurant runs a ton of specials, including different daily deals and a Burger of the Month.

Clearly, there is no shortage of best in show beef in this city!

34. BATTLE ROYALE

Swords are drawn in this fight to the death for the restaurant with the best pizza in Cleveland: Dewey's Pizza vs. Angelo's Pizza.

Dewey's Pizza, with its thin crust, explorative ingredients, and signature salads makes the first strike. Dewey's sets itself apart with its pizza window for spectators to watch the process, along with its legendary list of specialty pizzas. Dewey's prides itself on incorporating healthy, organic ingredients, and letting customers split their pizza into two different flavors, no matter how complicated your order is. As a former employee there, I can tell you that the porky fig and the green lantern are truly one of a kind (insiders tip: substitute the mushrooms on the green lantern for chicken, you won't be disappointed).

Angelo's returns the challenge though, with its superb execution of more traditional ingredients, and a thick crispy on the outside, soft on the inside crust. While Angelo's may be a little less wild than Dewey's, it has still perfected its craft and can be a great place to order a good, old fashioned pepperoni pizza. Angelo's Baked Potato Pizza is my personal favorite.

Located just down the street from each other in Lakewood, try out both of these places and choose your side in this pizza rivalry!

35. TREATS AND TRAINS

All aboard!

So you may not be able to grab a ticket to ride here anymore, but I would argue this fresh food marketplace housed in a 100 year old train station offers an even better experience. This community hub brings all the cultures of the city together. There's few places that will make you feel more like a local than the West Side Market. Clevelander's swell with pride whenever it's mentioned, and it's always a feature of Cleveland souvenir t-shirts, posters, dishes and everything in between. You'll also feel good shopping at this market, as all the stands are small , family owned businesses, most of which have been loyal to the West Side Market for decades. This marketplace is only open on Monday, Wednesday, Friday, and Saturday before 2:30 PM, and it offers a mix of made to order foods and more grocery store-esque items like meats, cheeses, fruits and vegetables.

The West Side Market is like a crowded maze. It has great energy and culture, but it can be tough to choose from the many options. If you're looking to order yourself a bite to eat at the West Side Market, find your way to the Cleveland Bagel Lady or Crepes de Luxe. If you are looking to plan yourself a picnic at one of the local parks, the West Side Market is a great place to pick up food to grill, and produce to eat with it! Finally, don't leave the West Side Market without indulging in one of the many bakery stands. Outside of the actual food, the West Side Market is a place that will give you a true feeling for the rich and diverse community that Cleveland has to offer...this is definitely worth a stop.

Eat Like a Local

36. LAKE ERIE IS GREAT

Cleveland is right on the shore of a world famous landmark: Lake Erie! With your supplies from the West Side Market or a local grocery store, a picnic at one of the local beaches is a great way to spend an afternoon, free of charge. If you are hoping enjoy the beach during your barbecue experience, then your best bet would be either Huntington Beach or Edgewater Park.

Huntington Beach is located in the suburb of Bay Village. With pavilions, picnic tables and grills, this is a great place for a family afternoon. Huntington is probably the largest beach in the Cleveland area, with swimming as an option, and it is surrounded by a small park that offers a great place for a leisurely stroll. This is a great place for some family fun!

Edgewater Park is closer to the city and has a smaller beach, but much more open park space. Edgewater is not only a great place for a picnic, but offers the field space for frisbee, football or any other lawn sports that need some space. Additionally, Edgewater Park is very pet friendly, and offers about three miles worth of recently renovated walking paths that offer plenty of room for pets to get their exercise.

Either way, both of these parks offer a beautiful Great Lakes experience that you shouldn't leave Cleveland without!

37. LESS BEACH, MORE LAKE

If you are looking for a lakefront experience, but would rather avoid the sand in your food, than your best bets are going to be Lakewood Park or the Pier Downtown.

Lakewood Park is located in its namesake Lakewood, one of Cleveland's most up and coming suburbs. A highlight of this park is its beautiful brick boardwalk that offers a one of a kind view of the lake and the Cleveland skyline. This park also has volleyball courts, a skatepark, and open field space that are all open to the public. Another great place for families, Lakewood park is a great place for a barbecue and relaxations. A local secret is to head to Lakewood Park around sunset, and take a seat on the

Eat Like a Local

Solstice Steps, which are specifically designed to offer a breathtaking view of a beautiful sunset every day. This daily occasion usually draws a crowd and ends in a round of applause once the sun finally sinks (very cheesy, but heartwarming nonetheless).

Alternatively, the Cleveland Pier is a much more urban hotspot but offers an equally great view. A great place to bring a blanket and eat a sandwich from a local shop downtown while taking in the vast beauty of Lake Erie. You might even catch a proposal at this popular engagement spot! Located on the northernmost part of 9th Street, right by the Browns Stadium and the Rock and Roll Hall of Fame, the Cleveland Pier is the best place downtown to really see the lake!

38. HIKIN' AND BIKIN'

You may have heard the rumors about Cleveland. Yes, our river did get catch on fire once. However, since that fateful day, we have changed our habits and our nickname of The Forest City has been living up to its name ever since! Cleveland has The Metroparks: a massive series of reservations that are located within different parts of the city. For those looking for the afternoon walk and picnic, go to The Rocky River Reservation! The area has plenty of picnic tables, grills, and even a playground for your needs. A spectacular view of Rocky River is also included for free!

Now, some of you may be thinking, that sounds too easy. I came here to get some type of workout in! Fear not, my friend. One of our towpaths runs from Cleveland to Akron. The trail in total is over 90 miles long! As you ride along the towpath, there will be restaurants to stop at, like Yours Truly or Winking Lizard. Plan on making a day out of this one! And if you do make it down to Akron, buy yourself a cold adult beverage. You have earned it!

39. A PARK FOR PICASSO'S

As you may have noticed from above, the modern and bustling West Side has activities galore to entertain a park lover, but the more historical East Side should not be forgotten and the highlight of this area has to be the diverse suburb of Cleveland Heights. I spent my college years living in Cleveland Heights and the winding streets and brick buildings will always hold a special place in my heart. If you are looking to take your picnic out to this romantic town, Cain Park should be your destination. Cain Park is a summer performing art park, with two outdoor theatres and an indoor Art Gallery to give you something to do after enjoying your lunch or evening barbecue. The park hosts a number of theatre productions, concerts, and dance companies and is a bustling center for entertainment in the summertime. Additionally, if you want to plan your trip around an event, the park hosts a nationally recognized art festival every July that brings in many local and out of town artists. On any weekend though, this park offers a unique entertainment experience that is worth the trip out to the East Side!

40. FALL IN LOVE WITH THE FALLS

Chagrin Falls is a suburb about 25 minutes or so outside central downtown. As you may have guessed by its name, a highlight of this quaint little town is the river and waterfall at the city's center! Although the Maid of the Mist won't be seen cruising through this waterfall, it is still a site to see nonetheless. An insider's tip from my hairdresser, a native of Chagrin Falls: make sure to grab some popcorn from The Chagrin Falls Popcorn Shop. She claims it's the best snack to take on your scenic walk through the falls. After enjoying what Mother Nature has to offer, take advantage of the window shopping that borders the river, especially Fireside Book Shop and Chagrin Cards and Gifts!

41. FOOD TRUCKS

Time is our greatest resource

So maybe I got a little too philosophical on you there for a second, but I know as a traveller, I often feel like I'm on a tight schedule to get all the sights in. If you're looking for some food on the go, the cleveland food truck scene provides a quick meal and an experience, all in one. If you are in Cleveland between May and September, the city hosts a circulating variety of food trucks every Wednesday in an event known as Walnut Wednesday. A great way to get a feel for the community, this is a little known event that will really make you feel like a local. If Wednesday is a packed day for you but the food truck idea still sounds appealing, the Lakewood Truck Park is a permanent food truck collection that is open every day, with different truck options offered each week. At Lakewood Truck Park, you can either eat your meal at the tables located within the park, or take your chosen delicacy on a walk through Lakewood. A great way to support the locals, for some outdoor food on the go, make a stop at one of these unique collections of small businesses!

42. EXPLORE THE SHOPPING SCENE

There really is no better one stop shop in Cleveland than Westlake's Crocker Park. This large outdoor shopping mall has all of your favorite name brands, with some local shops thrown in there as well. With over 130 stores, you really can shop till you drop, and when you're finished, there are restaurants galore to satiate your hunger. Your meal choices are bountiful at Crocker Park, but if you're finding yourself with a little sensory overload, let me lend you a hand... Aladdin's Eatery. I'll even narrow down the menu for you and tell you that the Chicken Curry Pitza is unforgettable, and make sure you order a side of hot sauce to dip your pita in. I'm not usually one for anything spicy, but even I can't resist this particular blend. To top it all off, in the summer, Crocker Park runs evening concerts from local musicians, with the performances located right outside Aladdin's! Shopping, entertainment and delicious food...could you ask for anything better?

43. FEEDING THE BODY AND THE SOUL

*"Art washes away from the soul
the dust of everyday life."*

Pablo Picasso

An afternoon at the award winning Cleveland Museum of Art, just as Picasso once said, will leave your soul feeling clean and calm. I have spent many an afternoon as both a teenager and an adult roaming the many exhibits of the museum and discovering something new every time. One of the best parts about this museum is that it is free of charge to the public! In addition to the wide range of art the museum offers on a consistent basis, they have seasonal exhibitions that often bring in world famous artwork.

Lunch at the museum is also an option with the attached Provenance Cafe, which includes lunch, dinner and snack options all made in its open style kitchen. The menu options at the restaurant, just like the art in the museum, are globally inspired and rich in variety. The restaurant is located right in the center of the museum, so you really feel like you are part of the setting while you enjoy your meal.

44. PLATES AND PUNCH LINES

Laughter is the most important meal of the day...or is that breakfast? Either way, you don't want to let your trip go by without getting a good hearty laugh in, and the best place to do that is at Pickwick and Frolic. This dinner restaurant and martini bar is combined with a popular basement comedy theatre: Hilarities Comedy Club. Pickwick features American rustic cuisine and has garnered numerous awards and affirmations for its martinis. The conjoined Hilarities Comedy Club hosts local and big name comedians, at a very reasonable price. The club has multiple shows running every night and you can order online or buy tickets at the door. This comedy club offers a cozy and connected atmosphere, that brought me to the club weekly for a year or so. If you're looking for dinner and a night out, this is my absolute favorite!

Eat Like a Local

45. END THE DAY ON BROADWAY

Leave the leg breaking to the actors with a visit to Cleveland's Playhouse Square! Fun fact (that all of us Clevelanders love to brag about): Playhouse Square is actually the second largest theatre district in the nation, only second to that of New York City. I would highly recommend seeing a show, but even if that is not an option, a walk through the square is definitely worth it, with the highlight being the giant chandelier which (another fun fact) is the world's largest outdoor chandelier. As you can see, the Cleveland Theatre District is shattering records for you to witness, take pictures, and tell your friends about.

If you're looking to sit down for a bite to eat near this landmark, Cibreo is probably your best bet. With traditional Italian food and an upscale vibe, Cibreo is a great introduction to the district before you see the characters get into action. If you want to skip the food and just snag yourself a quick drink instead, then the little in size but high in quality Parnell's Pub will definitely deliver. This tiny pub always offers great community, conversation and sometimes even some live music! Whatever you choose to do, a stop at Playhouse Square will be sure to make your day a success.

46. FREEZE BABY

There is no shortage of ice cream here in CLE. There's tons of your average chains, but if you want a real taste of Cleveland cream, my top 3 recommendations would be Mitchell's Ice Cream, Sweet Moses, or Piccadilly Artisan Creamery.

Mitchell's is our most well known ice cream chain, with its sleek and modern home base located in Ohio City, but there are about a dozen smaller shops scattered throughout the surrounding suburbs. Mitchell's hand crafts their ice cream at their store in Ohio City, where you can also watch them work their magic during your visit!

In contrast, Sweet Moses, located in Gordon Square, will take you on a blast to the past with its 1950's style design and service style. Upon walking into the shop, you will hear classic oldies playing through the sound system, pin striped high chairs along the ice cream and staff dressed as if you are at a Johnny Rockets in 1955. The menu features creamy homemade ice cream, old fashioned ice cream sodas, malts and much more!

Finally, if you are more of a frozen yogurt kind of person, Piccadilly Artisan Creamery is your target spot. Located both Downtown and in Cleveland Heights, Piccadilly is constantly experimenting with new and exciting flavors and topping to satisfy every frozen yogurt fiend.

No matter what kind of ice cream experience you are looking for, you will be sure to find it in this city!

47. DONUT FORGET THE DONUTS!

Sunday mornings call for a little Sunday indulgence and for me that means a freshly baked doughnut.

Here in CLE, the best place to get yourself a warm and doughy treat would be either Becker's Bakery in Fairview or Brewnuts in Gordon Square. Beckers is a family owned shop with an in house bakery. Get there early and you can get your doughnut warm out of the oven. If you are looking for a little more adventurous with your doughnut experience, check out the energetic Brewnuts Bar located in Gordon Square. Sporting a combination of beer, coffee, and beer infused doughnuts, kill two birds with one stone with this eclectic bakes and brews experience.

Do not (donut) forget to check these places out!

48. CUTE LIL' (OR BIG) CUPCAKES

If you're not quite into the breakfast bakery scene, but still want a fresh out the oven sweet treat, you may want to give a local cupcake a try! Cleveland has a cupcake for any appetite. If you're looking to keep your sweet snack small, pick yourself a beautiful, artfully crafted treat at a Cookie and a Cupcake on West 25th in Ohio City. This little, family owned bakery puts heart and soul into all of their treats, and offers more than just cupcakes, but other baked gods as well.

If you've got a big appetite or want something to share, drop by Colossal Cupcakes on for a rich and indulgent masterpiece. A tiny shop located on the bustling Euclid Avenue, this can be a great place to grab a treat while exploring downtown. Colossal Cupcakes was one of my favorite luxuries when I was living at Downtown while attending college at Cleveland State. You can get your cupcake the classic way, or get crazy and have your favorite blended into a milkshake...take your pick!

49. TO ALL THE CHOCOHOLICS

I think it was Confucius who said, "A balanced diet is chocolate in both hands." Even if that is an error on my part, we have to assume the person had lived near a Malley's Chocolates at some point through their lives. The quality and variety of chocolates to choose from will honestly have you eating the balanced diet Confucious once spoke about! Malley's stores are scattered throughout most of the city, but the two to poke your head into are its Lakewood location and North Olmsted location. Both stores have many of the chocolates they make in stock and are equipped with an ice cream shoppe. The North Olmsted location is a real kids crowd pleaser with a chunk of its seating located on a spinning carousel. Caution: you may not know whether to get the chocolate or ice cream. However, if you are anything like me, you will just buy both!

Eat Like a Local

50. A TOWN WILLY WONKA WOULD BE PROUD OF

So you are not quite into donuts and cupcakes. Do you have a taste for something like sour gummy worms, bubblegum, or taffy? Well, look no further! Cleveland has the largest candy store (verified search result) in North America with b.a. Sweeties Candy Company. If you long for a taste of the past that is not sold in a grocery store, chances are high b.a. Sweeties will have what you are looking for! Located in Brooklyn, the company offers any type of candy that you can imagine. It also has a soda shoppe and 36 holes of mini-golf on the property. Perfect for a night out with your friends or family! This place truly feels like stepping into a Wonka Factory and you don't even need a golden ticket!

READ OTHER BOOKS BY CZYK PUBLISHING

Eat Like a Local- Oklahoma: Oklahoma Food Guide

Eat Like a Local- North Carolina: North Carolina Food Guide

Eat Like a Local- New York City: New York City Food Guide

Children's Book: Charlie the Cavalier Travels the World by Lisa Rusczyk

Eat Like a Local

Follow *Eat Like a Local on* Amazon.
Join our mailing list for new books
http://bit.ly/EatLikeaLocalbooks

Made in the USA
Monee, IL
15 January 2024